D1320725

Maths Around Us

# Counting in the City

Tracey Steffora

**www.raintreepublishers.co.uk**
Visit our website to find out
more information about
Raintree books.

**To order:**

☎ Phone 0845 6044371

▤ Fax +44 (0) 1865 312263

▧ Email myorders@raintreepublishers.co.uk

Customers from outside the UK please telephone +44 1865 312262

Raintree is an imprint of Capstone Global Library Limited,
a company incorporated in England and Wales having its
registered office at 7 Pilgrim Street, London, EC4V 6LB
– Registered company number: 6695582

Text © Capstone Global Library Limited 2011
First published in hardback in 2011
The moral rights of the proprietor have been asserted.

Edited by Rebecca Rissman, Tracey Steffora, and Catherine Veitch
Designed by Joanna Hinton-Malivoire
Picture research by Elizabeth Alexander
Production by Victoria Fitzgerald
Originated by Capstone Global Library Ltd
Printed and bound in China by Leo Paper Products Ltd

ISBN 978 1 406 22314 9
15 14 13 12 11
10 9 8 7 6 5 4 3 2 1

**British Library Cataloguing in Publication Data**
Steffora, Tracey.
Counting in the city. -- (Maths around us)
513.2'11-dc22

**Acknowledgements**
The author and publisher are grateful to the following for
permission to reproduce photographs: Alamy pp. 6 (© Danny
Manzanares), 7 (© Tim Jones), 9 (© Marmaduke St. John), 10
(© Mike Spence/Greece), 11 (© Jon Mikel Duralde), 16 (© A.
T. Willett), 21 (© Blend Images), 23 glossary – bin (© Jon Mikel
Duralde); iStockphoto p. 5 (© Rich Legg); Photolibrary pp. 4
(Lauree Feldman/Ticket), 14 (White Star / Monica Gumm/image-
broker.net); Shutterstock pp. 8 (© Johan Pienaar), 12 (© aGinger),
13 (© hans magelssen), 15 (© gary718), 17 (© SVLumagraphica),
18 (© A Davis), 19 (© SOMATUSCAN), 20 (© kkymek), 22 (©
Adisa), 23 glosssary – crane (© Johan Pienaar).

Cover photograph of colourful taxis in Thailand reproduced with
permission of Shutterstock (© think4photop). Back cover
photograph of school buses reproduced with permission of
Shutterstock (© hans magelssen).

# Contents

# In the city

Numbers are everywhere in the city.

Numbers help us to count.

Here are ten birds.

Here are nine boats.

Here are eight cranes.

Here are seven dogs.

Here are six bells.

Here are five bins.

Here are four windows.

Here are three buses.

Here are two fans.

Here is one river.

There are zero cars on the bridge.

There are many people on the pavement!

# Things in sets

Some things come in sets.

Bicycle wheels come in twos.

Traffic lights come in threes.

Fingers come in fives.

What can you count in the city?

# Picture glossary

**bin** container that holds rubbish or recycling

**crane** large machine with a swinging arm that picks up heavy objects

# Index

**Notes for parents and teachers**

**Before reading**

The ability for children to recognize numbers is not the same thing as them being able to understand the concept of number, or the quantity that each numeral represents. Gather 45 of the same object, such as pennies. Count from one to nine with a child, pausing at each number to place that quantity of the object in their hand and then having them remove the objects and line them in rows on a table. This will help give children a visual and tactile sense of each numeral.

**After reading**

Supply a selection of books or magazines that contain urban scenes and have children hunt for objects to count. You can then have children contribute their findings to a large class chart or create counting books of their own. This activity can also be adapted to your own neighbourhood or community.